The Human Body

The Skeletal System

CHECKERBOARD SCIENCE LIBRARY

THE HUMAN BODY

Kristin Petrie MS, RD • ABDO Publishing Company

visit us at
www.abdopublishing.com

Published by ABDO Publishing Company, 4940 Viking Drive, Edina, Minnesota 55435.
Copyright © 2007 by Abdo Consulting Group, Inc. International copyrights reserved in all
countries. No part of this book may be reproduced in any form without written permission from
the publisher. The Checkerboard Library™ is a trademark and logo of ABDO Publishing
Company.

Printed in the United States.

Cover Photo: Corbis
Interior Photos: Corbis pp. 1, 4, 7, 9, 10, 13, 20, 21, 22, 25, 29; © Educational Images/Custom
    Medical Stock Photo p. 6; © L.Birmingham/Custom Medical Stock Photo p. 11; Peter
    Arnold pp. 5, 18, 23, 27; Visuals Unlimited pp. 15, 16, 17, 19, 24

Series Coordinator: Heidi M. Dahmes
Editors: Rochelle Baltzer, Heidi M. Dahmes
Art Direction: Neil Klinepier

Library of Congress Cataloging-in-Publication Data

Petrie, Kristin, 1970-
    The skeletal system / Kristin Petrie.
        p. cm.
    Includes index.
    ISBN-10 1-59679-714-2
    ISBN-13 978-1-59679-714-7
    1. Human skeleton--Juvenile literature. I. Title.

QM101.P38 2006
612.7'5--dc22

                                                            2005049310

CONTENTS

AMAZING BONES!

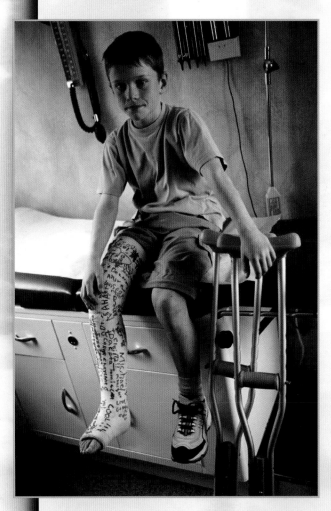

Have you ever broken a bone in your body? If you broke your leg, you may not have been able to stand on it. When a bone is broken, it can't do its main job. It can't hold you up!

Your skeletal system is made up of all of the bones in your body. Holding your body up is just one of the skeletal system's many jobs.

If you break a bone, your doctor will often set it in place with a plaster cast, a bandage, a sling, or a splint. The bone should not move during the healing process.

Your bones do undercover work, too. They act as armor for the delicate **organs** within your body, such as your heart.

Your bones are working hard right now, even if you are sitting still. They are holding you in an upright position. They are cradling your book. And your bones are growing.

Bones of every size make up your skeleton. The thigh bone is the longest and strongest bone. When it is done growing, it is about 20 inches (50 cm) long and 1 inch (2.5 cm) wide. The stirrup bone is the smallest bone. This is one of the three bones in your middle ear. It is only .07 inches (.18 cm) long!

YOUR SKELETON

Your skeleton is divided into two parts. First, there is the axial skeleton. This part includes your skull, spine, breastbone, and ribs.

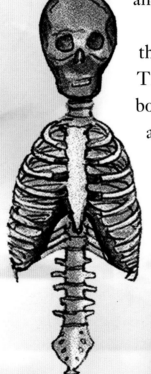

The other part is called the appendicular skeleton. This part includes all the bones that branch off of your axial skeleton. Your arms, legs, hands, and feet are all part of your appendicular skeleton.

An adult human's skeleton is composed of a whopping 206 bones! And, this skeleton is about 14 percent of the body's total weight.

Eighty bones make up the axial skeleton.

There are 126 bones in the appendicular skeleton.

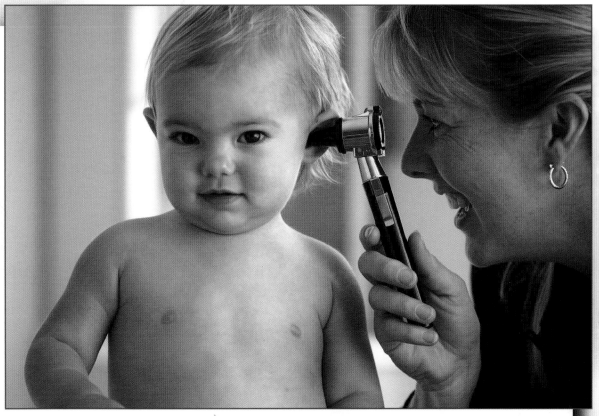

A baby's skull is made of soft cartilage plates. The spaces between these plates are referred to as soft spots.

    Is there a baby in your family? He or she has about 300 bones. You may be wondering what happens to all those bones. Well, they don't just disappear. As a baby grows, the bones fuse. In other words, they grow together.

So Many Bones!

We are all born with about 300 soft bones. Some of these bones are made of **cartilage**. These soft, bendable bones allowed you to stay comfortably squished inside your mother until birth.

As you grew from infant to toddler, your soft bones hardened. Eventually, hard bones replaced almost all of the cartilage. Just tap your head to see how hard these bones became.

As you know, your hard bones keep growing. You outgrow your pants, shirts, and shoes. Your bones will keep growing until you are about 25 years old.

You probably won't grow taller after this age. And, you'll stop outgrowing your shoes. But, don't send those bones to the museum yet! They will keep changing in different ways. Bones are made of living **tissue**. So, your bones will continue to change shape as long as you stay active.

Opposite page: Bones grow a lot during the childhood and teenage years. Maintain a healthy diet and exercise regularly so that your bones develop properly.

LAYERS OF BONES

Your bones are made of layers of living and nonliving materials. The outermost surface is called the periosteum. This layer is like an electric blanket. While an electric blanket holds wires, your periosteum holds blood vessels and nerves.

The cancellous layer of this femur bone is exposed. Cancellous bone is made up of a network of bone pieces called trabeculae.

Cancellous bone

Compact bone

Medullary cavity

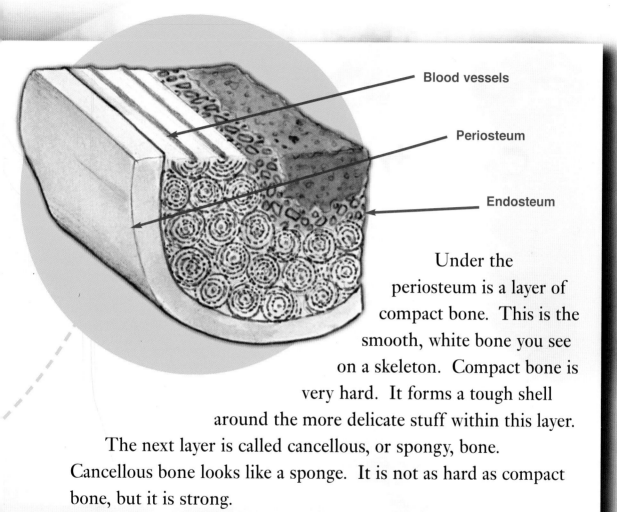

Blood vessels

Periosteum

Endosteum

Under the periosteum is a layer of compact bone. This is the smooth, white bone you see on a skeleton. Compact bone is very hard. It forms a tough shell around the more delicate stuff within this layer.

The next layer is called cancellous, or spongy, bone. Cancellous bone looks like a sponge. It is not as hard as compact bone, but it is strong.

Nerves and blood vessels run through all three layers of bone. These nerves and vessels also go to the delicate center of many bones. This is where bone marrow is found. The blood vessels within this marrow **nourish** spongy bone.

WHAT YOUR BONES DO

Hold on. That bone marrow sounds pretty important. Inside many of your bones, red bone marrow is busy making red and white blood cells. Red blood cells carry oxygen throughout your body. White blood cells help fight **germs** and keep you well.

What other important jobs does your skeletal system do? Obviously, your skeleton keeps you from being a heap on the floor. It's your body's hanger! This hanger also protects what's inside. For example, your skull protects your brain. And, your ribs protect your heart and lungs.

Your skeleton helps you move. To do this, your bones and muscles work together. Bones provide a surface for muscle attachment. And, bones work as **levers**. This means that when your muscles apply force to your bones, your body moves. Without bones and muscles, you would not be able to hit a volleyball over a net or climb a tree.

Your bones also store fat, phosphorus, and calcium. Calcium is necessary for a variety of bodily functions. Calcium builds strong bones and teeth. Your bones will pass calcium along to other body parts that need it. This way, there is always enough calcium circulating in the blood. But, problems occur if you don't get enough of this mineral in your diet.

You want to grow up big, strong, and healthy, don't you? Drink plenty of milk. It is a great source of calcium.

Types of Bones

You may not have known that your bones have so many jobs. But, you probably did know that bones come in different shapes and sizes. There are four shapes to your bones. These are long, short, flat, and irregular.

Long bones act as **levers**. They are found in your legs and arms. There are also some smaller long bones. These are found in your hands and feet.

Short bones are cube shaped. They are strong spongy bones covered by a layer of compact bone. There are short bones in your wrists and ankles.

Flat bones are thin and flat. They protect internal **organs**. And, they are attachment sites for muscles. Flat bones include your ribs and shoulder blades.

Irregular bones have many sizes and shapes. They support your weight, protect your spinal cord, and help you move. The vertebrae of your spine are irregular bones.

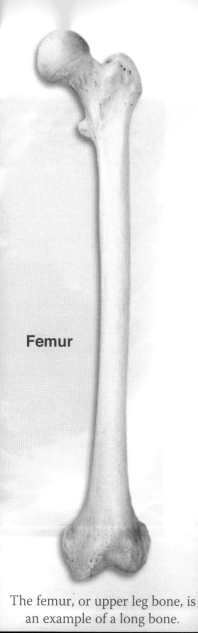

Femur

The femur, or upper leg bone, is an example of a long bone.

Calcaneus

This heel bone is a short bone found in the foot.

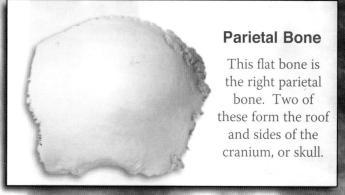

Parietal Bone

This flat bone is the right parietal bone. Two of these form the roof and sides of the cranium, or skull.

This irregular bone is the sphenoid. This bone is part of the skull base.

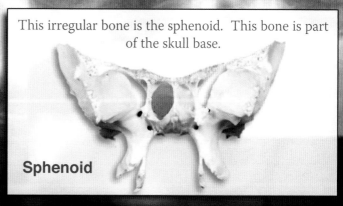

Sphenoid

YOUR SKULL

Your skeletal system has many parts. Let's start at the top with your skull. If you knock gently on your head, it sounds as though you are wearing a helmet. Thank goodness! Just inside this bony helmet is your squishy brain.

The skull has 22 bones. The top part is called the cranium. It is made of eight bones that protect the brain. These bones fit together like a puzzle. **Tissue** strips called sutures connect the eight bones together.

In the front of your skull are the facial bones. There are about 14 of these. Touch gently under your eye to feel the bone that makes your eye socket. Now run your finger from ear to ear to feel your jawbone. All of these bones give your face its **unique** shape.

The mandible, or lower jaw bone, is the only movable bone in the skull.

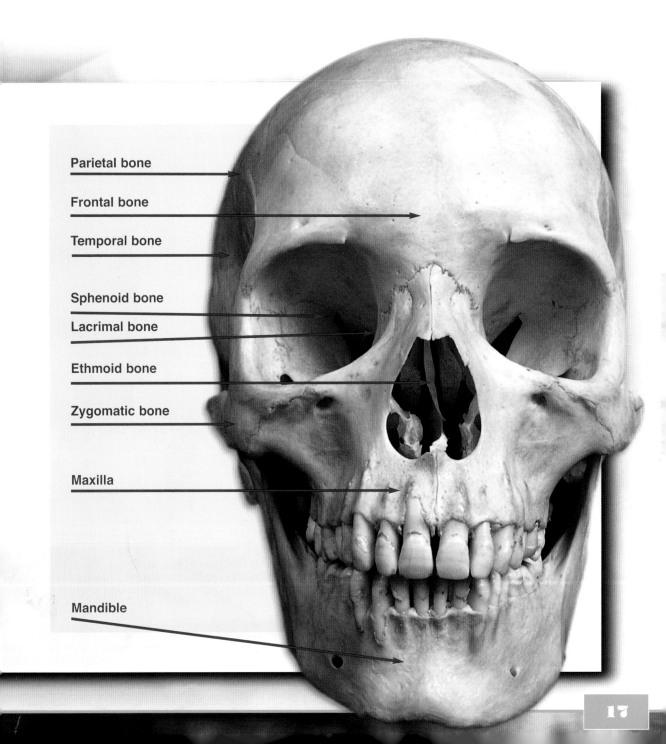

Parietal bone

Frontal bone

Temporal bone

Sphenoid bone

Lacrimal bone

Ethmoid bone

Zygomatic bone

Maxilla

Mandible

17

Your Spine and Ribs

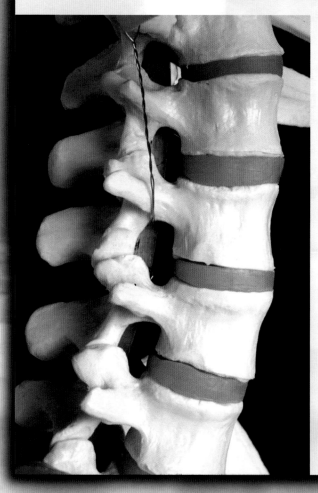

Now move your fingers to the back of your neck. This is where your spine begins. The spine is made of 26 bones called vertebrae. Vertebrae are like stacked blocks. And, each one is shaped like a ring.

The centers of the vertebrae rings make a safe place for your spinal cord. This bundle of nerves sends information from your brain to your body.

The average spine makes up about 40 percent of a person's height.

In between each vertebra are small disks made of **cartilage**. They keep your vertebrae from rubbing against one another. Cartilage is your body's own shock absorber. When you jump, thank those disks for cushioning your landing!

Your spine has an important job. It holds your ribs in place. Your rib cage is made of 12 pairs of flat bones. Each pair is connected in the back to your spine. The first seven ribs are also connected in the front to your breastbone, or sternum.

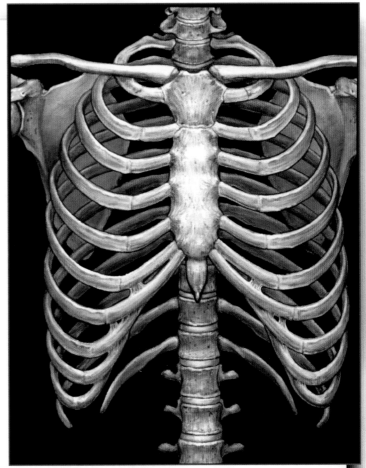

Your ribs form a protective covering for your heart, lungs, stomach, and liver.

YOUR ARMS AND HANDS

Have you hit your funny bone lately? If you have, you know it wasn't so funny! This uncomfortable tingling comes from a nerve that runs down your arm into your hand.

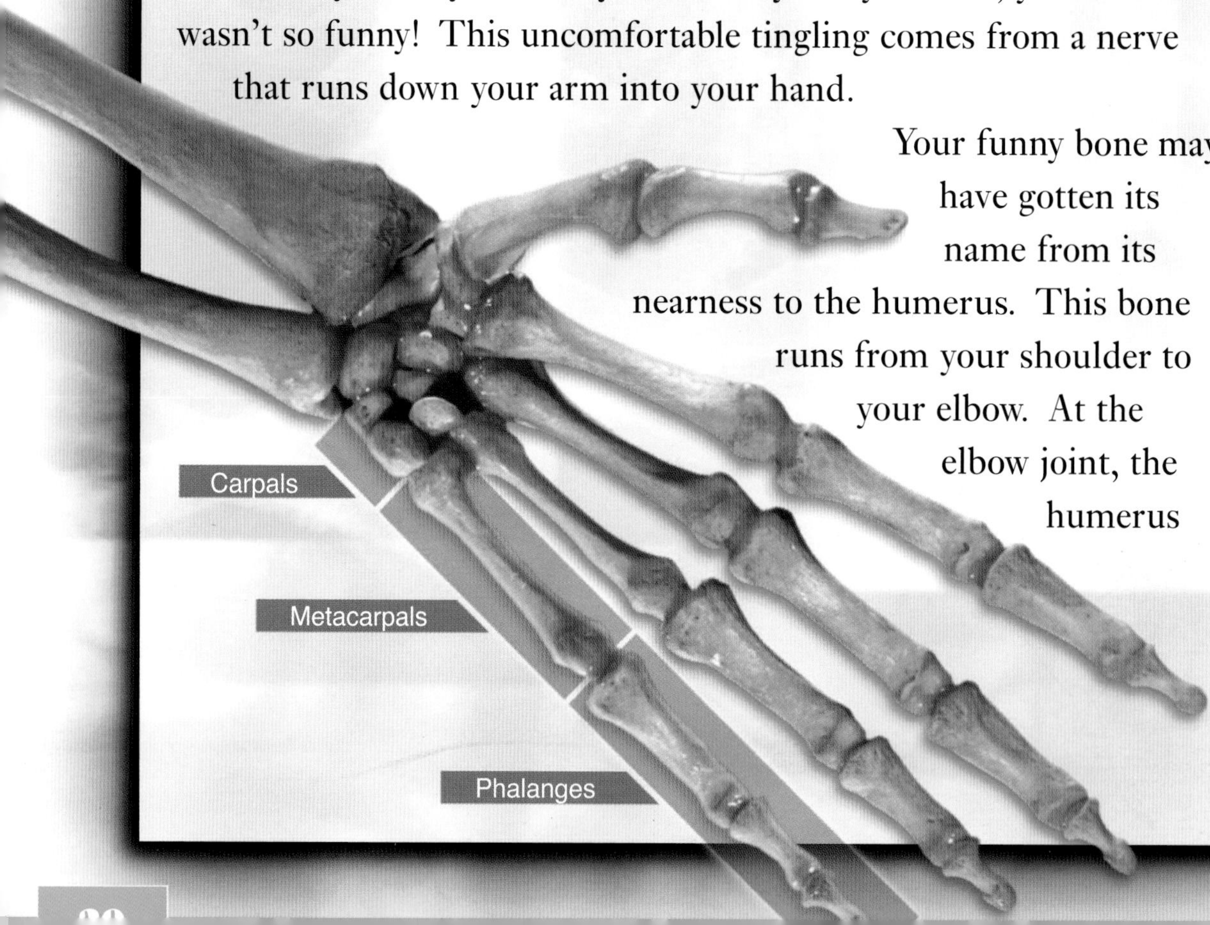

Your funny bone may have gotten its name from its nearness to the humerus. This bone runs from your shoulder to your elbow. At the elbow joint, the humerus

Carpals

Metacarpals

Phalanges

hooks up with the ulna and the radius. These are the two bones of your lower arm. You can feel these bones move if you place one hand on your forearm and twist.

At the base of the ulna and the radius is your wrist. Eight small bones make up this **flexible** part of your skeleton. Just look at how many ways you can move it!

The wrist leads to your hand. Together, the hand and the wrist have 27 bones. Every finger has three bones, but the thumb has just two bones. Five more bones are found in the center of your hand.

Your hands are the most flexible part of your skeleton. They are strong enough to grip heavy objects, such as your backpack when it is full of books. And, they are precise enough to allow you to write a letter.

Your Feet, Legs, and Hips

Now, look down at your feet. They will help you walk more than 80,000 miles (129,000 km) in your lifetime! Even your smallest toe works hard for you.

Altogether, there are 26 bones in each foot and ankle. These bones make your foot wide and almost flat. This structure helps you keep your balance, even on bumpy surfaces. Thank your toes and feet next time you walk to the mailbox.

Your leg bones are strong and large. Your fibula and tibia connect your ankle to your knee. Your femur connects your knee to your hip. All three of these bones carry your weight, so they are very strong.

Each foot has 14 phalanges, or toe bones. The big toe has two phalanges, but the other four toes have three.

Four more strong bones make up your pelvis. These four bones include the two large hip bones, the sacrum, and the coccyx. Your pelvis supports your spinal column. It also protects your bladder and intestines.

Your pelvis transfers your upper body weight to your legs.

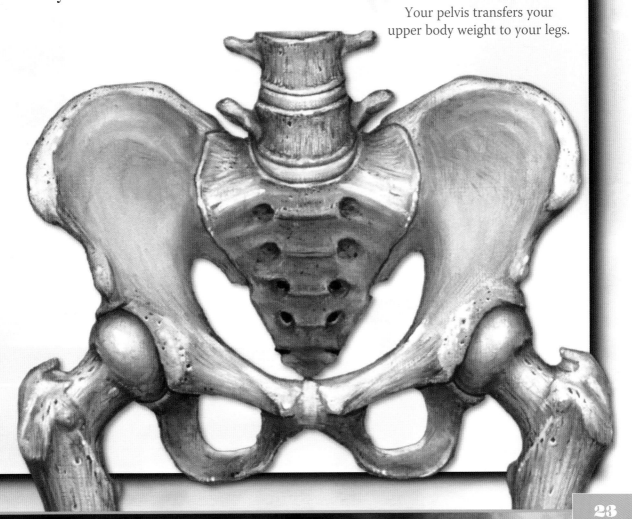

LIGAMENTS AND JOINTS

So many bones would be a mess without a good system to hold them together. Connective **tissues** called **ligaments** and **tendons** hold bones together. Ligaments and tendons are like ultrastrong rubber bands.

The place where two bones meet is called a joint. The most obvious moving joints are at your elbows and knees. These are called hinge joints.

Your shoulder joint is known as a ball-and-socket joint. So, you are able to move your shoulder forward, backward, and sideways in a rotating manner.

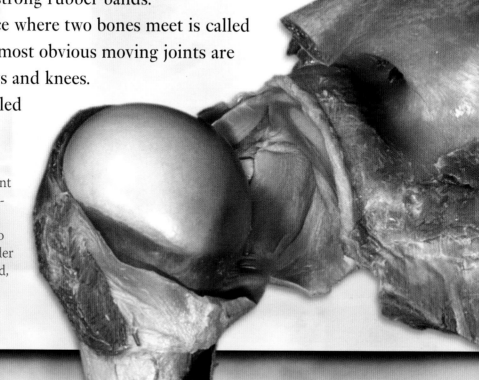

They work like a hinge on a door. Ball-and-socket joints are found in your shoulders and hips. They let you move your arms and legs in many directions.

Moving joints take a lot of wear and tear. So, your body makes a constant supply of synovial fluid. This natural "oil" keeps you from squeaking! It lets your joints move freely and smoothly.

Other joints move less but let you stay **flexible**. For example, the joints between your

Bones, muscles, and joints weaken without exercise. To remain flexible, start a fun exercise routine. Going for walks with your family or participating in karate are exciting options!

vertebrae allow you to twist and bend. Those in your ribs move just enough for you to take a big breath of air.

Bone Troubles

As you may know, even the strongest bones can break. When a bone breaks, it is called a fracture. A fracture can be a small crack where the bone does not fully break. Or, it can be a break where suddenly one bone becomes two.

Your bones know how to heal themselves. But don't test this out! Healing a broken bone is a long, painful, and boring process. When a fracture occurs, the body produces soft **tissue** to fill the gap and repair the break. As time goes on, the body deposits minerals in this soft tissue until it becomes hard.

Some diseases keep bones from doing their jobs properly. Osteoporosis is one of the most common bone diseases. Bone tissue thins, and bones become weak and **brittle**. This may be the result of too little calcium in a person's diet. As you know, your bones give away their calcium when the rest of the body needs it.

Arthritis causes pain at the joints. Sufferers experience tenderness, swelling, and limited movement of the joints. Arthritis affects more adults than children.

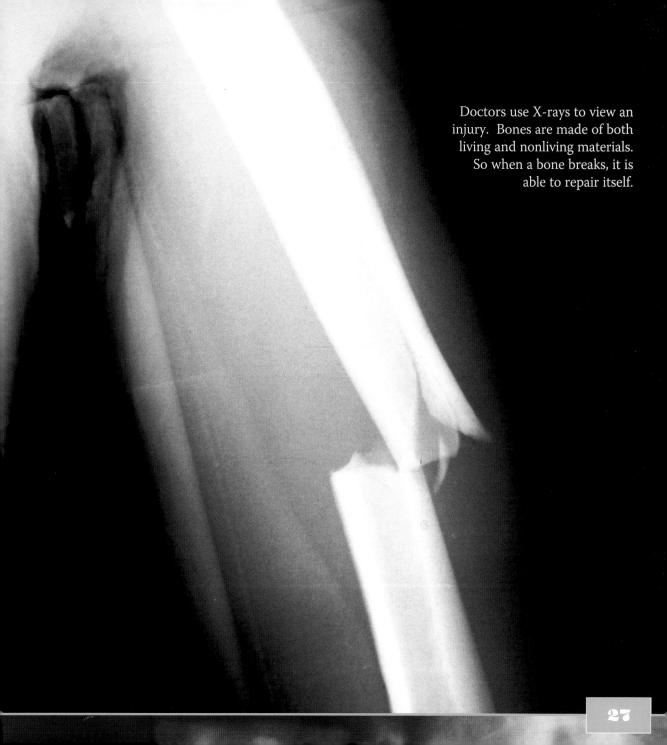

Doctors use X-rays to view an injury. Bones are made of both living and nonliving materials. So when a bone breaks, it is able to repair itself.

Caring for Your Skeleton

Now you know how important your skeletal system is. It's always working for you. So, be sure to take care of it. Eating healthy foods is the first step toward keeping your skeleton strong.

Remember that your bones love calcium. Drink milk and eat plenty of dairy products, such as cheese and yogurt. If you can't eat these foods, don't worry. Calcium is also found in leafy green vegetables, such as broccoli.

Exercise also helps keep your skeletal system in shape. Like muscles, bones gain or lose strength depending on how often they are used. Bones that don't get exercise lose mass and become weak. So, keep moving to keep your bones happy!

Protect your bones by being smart. Avoid dangerous stunts, think before you jump, and wear appropriate sports gear. Remember to always wear a helmet when biking, in-line skating, and skateboarding.

A helmet isn't the only protective gear that you should wear while skateboarding. Wrist, elbow, and knee pads are also important.

GLOSSARY

brittle – easily broken, cracked, or snapped.

cartilage – the soft, elastic connective tissue in the skeleton. A person's nose and ears are made of cartilage.

flexible – able to bend or move easily.

germ – a tiny living organism, especially one that causes disease.

lever – a rigid piece that sends and modifies force or motion from one point to another while rotating about a fixed point.

ligament – a band of strong tissue that connects two bones or cartilages or holds a body organ in place.

nourish – to feed or to help grow.

organ – a part of an animal or a plant that is composed of several kinds of tissues and that performs a specific function. The heart, liver, gallbladder, and intestines are organs of an animal.

tendon – a band of tough fibers that joins a muscle to another part, such as a bone.

tissue – a group or cluster of similar cells that work together, such as a muscle.

unique – being the only one of its kind.

SAYING IT

appendicular - a-puhn-DIH-kyuh-luhr

cartilage - KAHR-tuh-lihj

coccyx - KAHK-sihks

fibula - FIH-byuh-luh

osteoporosis – ahs-tee-oh-puh-ROH-suhs

periosteum - pehr-ee-AHS-tee-uhm

suture - SOO-chuhr

synovial - suh-NOH-vee-uhl

tibia - TIH-bee-uh

vertebrae - VUHR-tuh-bray

WEB SITES

To learn more about the skeletal system, visit ABDO Publishing Company on the World Wide Web at www.abdopub.com. Web sites about the human body are featured on our Book Links page. These links are routinely monitored and updated to provide the most current information available.

INDEX